Oscar
The Extraordinary
Hummingbird

Revised and Expanded Edition

Lisa Worthey Smith

Kerysso Press

ISBN-13: 978-1-704806-59-4

Reviews

"A tender story of love by surprise. The injured bird placed right in the path of a lover - a compassionate woman who understood and had to learn to speak "hummingbird" to communicate.

The story is heartwarming, but there is also sadness. In the end, "joy cometh in the morning."
James Miller, author of the Cody Musket series

"Like reading Liz Curtis Higgs."
Melanie

"Lisa has the rare gift of seeking and finding the hand of God in all of life's experiences, whether in her backyard or on her back in a hospital bed! Not only does she share the lessons she's learned from life and the Word of God but in the last section of the book she teaches one how to glean these truths for oneself in a study of scripture.

I will read this book many times over and consider it one of my treasures!"
Leslie, Amazon reviewer.

"What a wonderful book of stories showing God's love for us through nature. Our Lord and Savior teaches us so much if we take the time to observe and listen.

Lisa has an amazing talent of being able to relate those lessons through this book. I highly recommend it!
Teri, Amazon reviewer

"Such a treat to take yourself away from daily stresses. Oscar the Extraordinary Hummingbird gives the reader lovely stories and reminds you of the wonderful beauty of Gods creation and the lessons we learn as we are still and listen.

Very well written and will look forward to more."
Penny, Amazon reviewer

"This is a very inspirational book! It has changed the way I think about all of God's creations!"
Hilda, Amazon reviewer

Dedication

To all who have experienced
difficulty,
joy
or sorrow
may the hand of God
be evident to you,
strengthen you,
and guide you.

Foreword

I t takes a special eye to capture something beautiful in a painting or picture. It takes a special talent to compose and create beautiful music, poetry, and prose. However, it takes a spiritual gift to be able to see the work of God in the everyday events of one's backyard. Lisa Smith's *Life in My Father's World* captures the work of God, and provides powerful illustrations of the Word of God in ways that are encouraging and inspiring.

I've fed hummingbirds for years, but never saw what Lisa was able to see in caring for Oscar. I've seen goldfish, but never learned what Lisa learned from *Life in the Pond*. Her observations of *Life in the Garden* are brilliant, as she looks at flowers, seeds, and even predators from a biblical view. She records powerful lessons learned from ordinary events in the life of God's creation, lessons that illustrate biblical truths and teach us of God's care for even the sparrow that falls to the ground.

If you are struggling with life, if you are experiencing sorrow, if you are discouraged, or dealing with doubt—this book will encourage you, inspire you, and teach you of God's constant and abiding presence in your life. It will help you to see the Lord in ways you may never have seen Him before. I found the book to be a great blessing, and I pray you will find the blessings you need in your life as you see *Life in the Father's World* through the eyes of one who herself has faced great challenges in this life---and yet sees the presence and power of God. Lisa is an outstanding student of the Bible, lives out her faith everyday with courage and determination, and seeks to share her lessons with others. You will enjoy this book---and it will change your perspective on God's creative work, and how He works in your life.

Walter Blackman
Pastor,
East Highland Baptist Church, Hartselle, AL

Preface

This collection of stories includes the chronicle of a tiny hummingbird and the unlikely friendship he and I shared. Through the time we spent together, God used Oscar to teach me many things about

life,

suffering, and

joy in the midst of it all.

I remain amazed that He chose this itty-bitty bird and so many precious, yet seemingly insignificant, things within His Creation to demonstrate such profound spiritual truths to me and am delighted to share these simple stories with you.

May you always take time to see God
In the little things.
They may become your
biggest treasures!

Lisa Worthey Smith

Acknowledgments

"Thank you" is hardly enough to express my gratefulness to my dear high school sweetheart with whom I am living out our "happily ever after" of forty years and counting. My Mr. Tall Dark and Handsome has been by my side through thick and thin and, when it looked like my life was nearly over, minute by minute.

"Thank you" could never be enough to those who gave me my very life. My parents have long been my biggest cheerleaders.

"Thank you" is far from adequate to so many friends and family who have encouraged the writing of these pages, so I pray that you each know my heart and the gratefulness within it.

Thank you, Melanie, for helping my words clearly present the story.

Most of all, thanks be to my precious God for all He has done and continues to do to draw me nearer to Himself! I pray that within this little book

"the words of my mouth and the meditation of my heart
be acceptable in Your sight, O LORD,
my rock and my Redeemer."[i]

Introduction

All the tales within this book are true. The simple parable-type lessons offered here about life in my Father's world have touched my soul, and I pray that your heart will likewise be enriched by reading them.

Inside you will become acquainted with Oscar, the sweetest little hummingbird you ever could meet, along with some fishy characters you will stroll with me through the beauty and splendor of the garden. Together we will explore patterns and truths found in Creation which point us to a deeper understanding of our Creator.

As you open the pages, please take your time to savor each bite. Then, I pray you will vividly see the evidence of God surrounding you. As you do, please share some morsels with those around you. After all, life is full of peace and joy when we witness the hand of God at work, and who doesn't need a little extra peace and joy!

Lisa Worthey Smith

Oscar the Extraordinary Hummingbird

Lisa Worthey Smith

Kerysso Press

Lisa Worthey Smith

A Tiny Treasure

When I first spotted the mysterious wad, grand hopes of discovering some sort of little treasure filled my brain. I am familiar with the ending of the curious cat, but was compelled to investigate nonetheless. By the size and shape it might even be an owl pellet! Because owls have no teeth with which to chew their meals, they swallow them whole. They also—uhm—"release" the undigested portion whole, in a pellet form, just about the size of this suspicious little gem. As I drew closer to the twisted little glob, I realized it wasn't what I hoped for at all.

My heart sank. I reached down to the small hummingbird who apparently met an untimely demise. His little body was twisted in an unnatural position. His poor, tiny head had been stripped of all feathers on top and on one side, revealing only raw, purple and blue skin. Fishing line encircled his mouth. Perhaps his injuries came as the result of a run-in with a weed-eater or lawn mower.

I gingerly lifted up the bruised and limp little bird and cradled him in the palm of my hand. His beauty amazed me. My heart ached for him and the suffering he must have endured.

As he rested in my palm, I became aware of a faint, rapid thumping against my hand. A heartbeat!

Thankful for the opportunity to comfort him in his final moments of life, I ever so gently stroked his broken little body and brought him close to my face while whispering, "God knows when a sparrow falls[ii], and He knows all about little hummingbirds, too." Realistically, it was more a prayer to comfort me than an expectation that he actually understood what I had said to him.

Fighting back tears, I blew softly into his face to let him know he was not alone.

He blinked his eye—the one that wasn't swollen shut. Yes, he heard me. He knew I was there with him and perhaps he understood that God was as well.

I don't claim to know how much animals understand. I do know my responsibility, according to the Word of God in the book of Genesis, is to "rule[iii] over (or have dominion over) the creatures of the earth." Surely this would include taking care of one who has fallen. God spared him long enough for me to comfort him a bit, and for that, I was grateful. I just absolutely love the way God works and have found that His timing is perfect, always.

Continuing to bathe him with my warm breath, I slowly and as tenderly as possible, began to untangle him from the fishing line in and around his mouth to give him as much comfort as possible. He blinked again and tried to lift his poor, bruised, and bald little head.

As the untangling progressed, it became apparent that the "line" was his tongue. Poor fellow! Bless his sweet little heart. He must have wondered, *Why is this woman pulling on my tongue?* He was having a bad enough day already without me tugging on his tongue, of all things.

I chuckled at the absurdity and apologized ."Sorry about that, little guy."

Gradually, as he regained consciousness, his tongue retracted into its proper place, and he looked at me, with his one good eye—not with fear, but rather with curiosity.

I continued to examine him for injuries and found that one wing was not in the correct position, and a tiny spot of blood was on the front of his neck. So, still holding him in one hand, I took a paper towel with the other hand and dampened one corner, folding it over to make a swab to lightly sponge his wounds. I stroked and tucked the tiny wing back into the proper position.

By now, he was more conscious than not but, still too weak to resist my "mothering." He didn't have the strength to fly, but he did seem content to rest in the warmth of my hand.

Because most acquaintances begin with an exchange of names I— not knowing his hummingbird name— decided to call him Oscar. You know, like the Grouch. Both are green, a mess, and more than a little grumpy. It seemed to fit.

Oscar. Bald but alive.

With injuries this severe, I feared he would perish before I could document this precious moment. So, while he was still alive, I took a few pictures of Oscar in my hand. I marveled at the opportunity to hold such a small, magnificent creature. I continued to assure him of my intention to help him to the very best of my ability. He was truly a pitiful sight - tiny, helpless, bruised, and bald - but alive!

Although I tried to clean the blood speck from his neck, I could not, and he grew tired of my trying, so I used the wet swab to try to soothe the bruising on his raw and battered scalp and face. From the size of the swelling and bruising on his scalp, he had to have one whopper of a headache. That little head was going around in circles as if he were watching a Ferris wheel. Perhaps he had a concussion.

Because of his dizziness and lack of ability to control that wobbly head, instead of offering him the hummingbird feeder, I dipped a baby spoon into a sugar-water solution and nudged his beak with it. He licked the one drop from the bottom of the spoon and then licked his lips (beak), realizing it was good. Good indeed! His tongue still worked and he was able to take some liquid nourishment.

He listened to my words (well, indulge me a bit, it seemed that way to me), appeared to understand that I was trying to help, and seemed to be comforted by my efforts. If nothing else, he wasn't alone. Oscar was a strong, brave little bird who wanted to live, and I wanted to help him live.

Oscar sipping sugar water from a spoon.

The Start of a New Life

As Oscar gained enough strength to hold himself upright a little, it was apparent that the injured wing was still dangling much lower than the other and at the wrong angle, despite my continuing to put it back in place. Was it broken or dislocated? I couldn't imagine how to set such a tiny wing. If I tied gauze around him, would he be able to breathe properly? Would he hurt himself even more trying to get it off? Even if the gauze worked, I might still set the wing in the wrong place and prevent him from ever flying again. I needed help.

I called a local avian veterinary office. Because Oscar was a wild animal and not a pet, they did not offer treatment but supplied me with the phone number of a local wildlife rehabilitator. I called the rehabber's home but found she was at the hospital with her son who was very sick. I offered up a prayer for her and her family and realized I was on my own after all.

I started with an attempt to think of a way to house him. A cardboard box and a towel could serve as his bedroom. I thought it was perfect! Oscar was not impressed. He preferred to be in my hand, and let his preference be known with squawks and jumps when I tried to introduce him to his temporary new apartment. Maybe it was just the warmth, but it made me smile to think that I had earned his trust.

All his cousins who have stopped by our house for sips of sugar-water through the years, have darted off hastily when either my husband or I approached them. Oscar likewise should have been terrified to be restrained by this enormous creature who could have eaten him in one bite. So, I held him cupped in one hand and lightly covered with the other. He deserved a little spoiling after the day he had endured. Safe and warm in my hand he fell asleep. I had to refrain myself from jumping up and down at this marvelous opportunity, to have a hummingbird fall asleep in my hand!

As you can imagine, I relished that moment and held him like that for some time as he slept, absolutely thrilled to have such an amazing privilege! I couldn't help but see the beautiful picture of our heavenly Father holding us in His hand. Although He is the Almighty Creator

See Oscar's tiny feet?

of the vast universe and is all-powerful, He still tenderly holds us in the palm of His hand. There we can find rest[iv] and be completely safe and secure.[v] What a blessing to experience this reminder of His love and care for me!

Finally, after little Oscar was calmed and convinced to spend the night in the box, I prayed that he would not be frightened, and that he would survive the night.

He did.

The next day, my husband and I went to a local store to print out the photographs that were taken in those first hours. As the photos came out of the printer slot, we saw Oscar captured on film in all his glory. They were somewhat out of focus, and some were hardly even recognizable.

While we were sorting through them, out of the blue, a lady walked behind us, then turned back toward us and asked, "Is that a hummingbird?" and informed us that she rehabilitates birds.

Did I mention that I just love God's perfect timing? It is no wonder that He is called the "on time God"!

Even before she told me her name, I suspected I already knew it and smiled.

She confirmed my suspicion. I let her know that I had prayed for her and her family just the day before.

She took a step back and shifted her gaze from the pictures to look at me again, wondering how I knew her and if she knew me. I explained that I had called her home the previous day to ask for help with the bird and was told about the situation with her sick son, then as a result had prayed for her and her family. She updated us with news that her son had just been released from the hospital, and she was at this store to pick up medication for him so that he could continue his recovery at home.

Though grateful for the prayers, the rehabber was a weary stressed mom. While interested in the well-being of Oscar, rather than taking in another patient at her house, she offered to show *me* how to take care of Oscar. Understandably, her priority would have to be taking care of her son.

That plan worked for me! I was eager and honored to learn how to help my newest little friend.

She took home the things her son needed, got him settled in, and then came to my house to meet Oscar. She inspected the little bird with the compassion of one who has spent a lifetime helping critters in distress.

The sunroom where I was caring for him was suitable after a few modifications. She came prepared with a print-out of detailed instructions on the proper care and feeding he would require and shared that with me. She told me about the special food he would need—otherwise, Oscar's kidneys would fail after forty-eight hours of a diet of only sugar water.

What a relief to know I wasn't alone after all. I had been given this incredible tiny feathered gift—a far better treasure than that for which I originally hoped—and now I was being equipped to take care of him.

Thus began my unlikely friendship with Oscar.

The Bachelor Pad

Because it is illegal to "keep" wildlife, I became a licensed wildlife rehabilitator and worked to learn as much as possible about how to properly care for him while he recovered. His home was upgraded from a cardboard box to an old aquarium with a screen over the top that included special light bulb that mimics actual sunlight for both his warmth and his health. They must have sunlight to thrive.

His little toes were designed to hold onto a little branch so I was shown how to make a perch using a wooden shish-ka-bob skewer stuck into inverted small plastic cup "bookends." He loved it!

His feeding needed to simulate drinking from a flower, and I learned how to rig up a syringe - no needle, just syringe - with small amounts of a liquid food which is high in protein (not just the sugar-water nectar most of us keep in our hummingbird feeders).

A large plastic cup was modified by cutting out openings for the syringe to pass through from back to front, and be at the appropriate height for him to access as if it were the neck of a flower. I even painted a flower around the front opening where he drank from the syringe "flower." I doubt that he recognized it was supposed to be a real flower, but thought it might help him realize the shape and colors of flowers that were the source of food and spend his recovery time in as near to the normal hummingbird habitat as possible.

I added a few inches of sand to his aquarium and buried some plants in it (think terrarium) for him to hide in, hop on and rub against. There were also places for fresh blooming flowers to be added as they were available. The sand was covered with paper. The terry cloth towel that I thought would be so comfortable on the floor of his home (carpet, if you will) had to be removed, otherwise his toes could become entangled. Why didn't I think of that?

That was just one of the many times I learned my way is not always the best, and my way can do more harm than good, no matter how well-intentioned. It is a good idea to consult with an expert, and my expert had raised many exotic birds and rehabbed many others. I was thankful for the tutoring and the tutor.

With a little creativity and imagination, a plastic lid from a sour cream container turned bottom side up and filled with a few tablespoons of water, served as a bathtub/pool. It didn't take long for him to discover this little watering spot. He jumped in and out of his personal lagoon over and over. He loved it! His very own bachelor pad with an indoor pool!

Because Oscar enjoyed his watering hole so much, I wondered if he might like a rain shower spa treatment too. A plastic bottle with a misting nozzle and warm water was used for the experiment. Well, to say "he liked it" is a grand understatement! Oh, what a deliriously happy bird!

I purposely aimed the spray into the pool area so that all the paper flooring wouldn't be soaked. After a couple of times he knew our routine, and when he spotted the mister, right away he would scurry down the perch toward the pool area and wait with joy for me to begin the spray.

He liked to dance in the mist by scooting a few steps to the left, then to the right, going in and out of spray. He put on quite an entertaining show, fluttering his clean, beautiful, and happy little wings, chirping (singing in the shower?) to his little heart's content. Every day he seemed so very grateful for the simple joy of a bath - as if he had been covered with mud and had never touched water before.

Oscar in his bachelor pad, with spa.

After each thorough soaking, Oscar loved to bask in the sunshine and preen until every feather was in its proper place. Maybe it was just the "proud Mom" in me, but it seemed to me that he grew more handsome and sparkled more and more every passing day.

How much more grateful am I that God can cleanse my deepest stains of iniquity. How glorious to be washed by my Creator who can see my sins (filth),[vi] and can clothe me in His righteousness.[vii] I can't clean myself, but must rely upon Him totally, akin to the way Oscar relied upon me.

I began to see God using Oscar to demonstrate His relationship to me. I found Oscar, chose to pick him up, cleaned him up, gave him food and shelter – a new life.[viii] It was different from his old life now as part of my family and dependent on me rather than himself. I began to see first-hand how God employs brokenness for the purpose of blessing.

Lisa Worthey Smith

Walking the Bird

As the days went by, I continued to hold him when he was cold, to speak to him with encouraging words, and to walk him—well, actually I walked and he rode on my pointer finger—outside to do hummingbird things. It was such a sweet thing to experience. All I had to do was to lower my hand into his aquarium house, and he would practically run over to hop onboard a finger for our outing.

When we approached a flower, he would lean toward it, as if he were the driver, to let me know where he wanted to stop. I wish I had recorded it for you! He liked to probe around and sip from flowers (phlox and hummingbird flowers were among his favorites) and experience the sun and wind on his wings, and even drink from the hummingbird feeder, just as if he had flown there all by himself. I always cheered him on by telling him "what a big bird he was" sitting there.

I was very proud of him, and he seemed to know it. He thought he was really something. He tried to take flight many times, especially if there was a little breeze. The bum wing didn't cooperate however, and therefore I dug him out of flowerpots and leaves many times. Still, I encouraged him to fly.

Rehabilitators do not have wildlife "pets." Our job is to help them through their trauma, whether injury or abandonment, and then release them to fulfill the rest of their lives as the deer, raccoon, squirrel, or in this case, the hummingbird, they were made to be. I am so grateful to know that my Father, Who loves me and designed me,[ix] will both be with me to encourage me to do what He created me to do and help me get back on track when I fail.

New head feathers began to sprout into a cute little spiked hairdo and the spot of blood on his neck turned out to be the beginnings of a ruby throat. He was growing into quite a handsome bird, and I reminded him of that every day. His previously swollen head and face now looked more normal and the head was not so wobbly. In the sunshine his feathers absolutely lit up as if he was bejeweled with sequins.

I rejoiced in the astounding beauty God had given this little creature. Consider the lilies of the field[x]... even Solomon (the richest king on earth) in all his glory was not attired in the spectacular beauty of this itty-bitty bird who some would consider inconsequential—except for me, of course. I knew he was special.

Although his head feathers returned and his ruby throat feathers grew in, his wing was still of little use to him despite my ongoing attempts to put it in place. He wasn't just injured, he was broken. Perhaps hummingbirds dream to fly freely to any flower in the field, to travel great distances and to sojourn continents, but I began to have serious doubts that Oscar would be able to fulfill such a life. How could he be the hummingbird he was meant to be without even being able to fly?

I wished that I had the means to explain to him that, while he might not be able to fulfill his hummingbird dreams of traveling to multiple continents and exotic locations, his presence in my life gave me such tremendous joy. Without hummingbird words, how could I possibly tell him that his disability gave me a better perspective on how God uses life circumstances to draw us nearer to Himself? I longed to find a way to show him how precious and beautiful he was, and how very blessed I felt to have a part in his life.

He really, REALLY enjoyed the outside excursions and began to demand to go with me. His room (our sunroom) is on the normal trail we take going from inside to outside, and he loved to go outside. So, he came to realize that when I came out, he might get to go out, too. Soon, when I came into his sight, he would jump down off the perch and lightly bounce up and down with hummingbird glee, following me from one end of the aquarium to the other, ready to hop onto my hand and go out.

Maybe, just maybe, I was a little (or a lot) guilty of spoiling him. He had a little trouble understanding that he didn't get to go out every time I did, and he didn't try to hide his disappointment. Eventually, if I had the nerve to pass by and didn't slow down to take him with me, his light bouncing turned into hopping and squawking in total disbelief, while furiously stomping his little feet at me! If you have ever witnessed a two-year-old toddler have a temper tantrum (here in the South, we call it "pitching a fit"), you have a good idea what it was like.

The audacity of this tiny bird not even as big as my finger demanding his way was not lost on me. A little bird, with a little pea sized brain (literally) was insisting that I give in to what he wanted when he wanted. It truly was a comical sight, this little guy weighing less than a penny pitching a full-blown hummingbird temper tantrum! Again, I offer my apologies for lack of video.

As a rule, I ignore temper tantrums from people or birds, but I did respect his enthusiasm and persistence. He really did not have to be demanding because I wanted to take him out as often as I could, just so he could enjoy Creation and I could enjoy his company.

God desires to give me even more good gifts than I desired to give Oscar,[xi] yet I have been guilty of stomping my feet at Him, demanding my way, my timing, my outcome. Maybe you have done that, too. God used Oscar to demonstrate my position to Him and how even more ridiculous it was for me to demand my way over His. I don't always like chastisement (well, actually, I don't ever like it), but I am grateful that He gently and lovingly shows me my foolishness toward Him.[xii] I do so love the way He works.

Oscar took such pleasure from being outside that I created a little outdoor room for him using a disposable plastic cake cover turned upside down. When I went out, he could get in this mobile bachelor pad and enjoy the outdoors, leaving my hands free to do other things. I still carried him by hand to the flowers for a sip. Actually, hummingbirds extend their tongues way down into flowers to retrieve ("lick," if you will) the nectar – along with any insects trapped within the sweet juice. Before you cringe, the insects add some protein necessary for their diet. It's a bird thing.

After he had a chance to explore a bit, I usually gathered a few blossoms and sturdy leaves to put in his outdoor spa so he could frolic on them on his own. When I sprayed a little water on them, Oscar literally rubbed against the leaves as if it were a washcloth for his face. You would think he had peanut butter on his sweet little cheeks that he just couldn't wipe off. He played around on the leaves and bloomers to his little heart's content with a joy you would just have to have witnessed to understand. I truly wish you could have seen it.

By now, I had learned that my precious little Oscar's injuries likely didn't come from a lawn mower but from other hummingbirds. While

I had seen hummers shriek at each other and fiercely fight in the air, I didn't realize that they would sometimes hold another bird down and mercilessly pluck out their feathers.

So, when Oscar and I were outside and I heard other hummers, I watched to see how he would react. At first, he stopped and quietly listened to the other hummers.

After several days he chirped a response back to them. Whether he was a victim of bullying or taught a lesson about infringing on another's territory, I will never know. When he chirped to them, I don't know if he remembered that day when he was attacked and forgave, or remembered and was afraid. I had no way to ask him, and he had no way to tell me.

Life can be hard, and our perception of memories can either make us grateful or hateful. I choose to think Oscar was willing to forego anger and give them another chance. Life is better when full of hope. Bitterness robs you of the blessings of the day.

"He who is slow to anger
is better than the mighty, and
he who rules his spirit,
than he who captures a city."[xiii]

Meeting Windy

My fellow rehabber had been working with a female hummer, Windy, that had a broken wing. We talked about the two solitary birds and decided they might enjoy living "happily ever after" together, so she brought Windy to join Oscar. If only I had recorded this on video.

Oscar, in his bachelor pad, watched with curiosity from one end of his perch (remember the shish-ka-bob?) as the rehabber came into the sunroom. He was always interested in watching people—perhaps he thought someone would take him on a field trip outside.

Windy was a somewhat edgy about being in an unfamiliar place and fluttered and squawked a bit. Oscar watched and listened, interested but patient. I introduced myself to Windy, then scooped her up with both hands for a proper face to face meeting. She gave me a good looking over and calmed down. I opened my hands and placed her on the opposite end of the perch from Oscar. The rehabber and I both hoped that it would not be a violent confrontation and stood ready to intervene if necessary.

It wasn't.

With his body frozen and only his eyes moving, he looked at her, then looked at me, looked at her, then looked back at me as if asking, *For me?* Our pastor has contemplated what Adam might have thought, seeing all the creatures, but none like him. Then when Adam awoke from his sleep (minus a rib) and saw the lovely creature God had created just for him, perhaps he had a *For me?* look in his eye. That *For me?* look is what I got that day from Oscar. He didn't know what to do, but he seemed to be in a state of marvel and wide-eyed amazement.

Windy, on the other hand, seemed to have an *Aha!* moment and immediately wanted to check out this handsome bird up close. So, she scooted two steps toward Oscar. Oscar promptly scooted two steps away. This continued until he came to the very end of that side of the perch.

I was still a bit fearful that Oscar might not appreciate a female in his bachelor pad but maintained hope that they might grow to like the idea of sharing a space. Considering Oscar's previous experience, I didn't blame him for being reserved, maybe even bashful.

Bashful was not in Windy's name or personality. She finally got close enough to touch him on the side with her beak. He looked the other way. That led to her touching her beak to his back, which he bristled about at first. We watched carefully and hovered over them, ready to intervene if a battle ensued. Trying to squeeze out another step away from this little girl and not finding any more room, he decided to nonchalantly ignore her as if this sort of thing happened to him every day. Finally, she crossed her beak over his, looked him eye to eye, and won him over.

We stared at the charming couple with both delight and relief. The rest, as they say, is history. They were side

My handsome bird on the right, with Windy.

by side most of the time thereafter. Even though they each had their own feeder syringe, often they would drink from the same one at the same time. They would snuggle up into a single little wad at night to sleep. They appeared to be happy. It seemed a nice pairing of two nice little birds which otherwise would not have survived, and they accepted each other, blemishes and all. It was a real treasure to behold.

God has provided me with things and events that I didn't expect or particularly like (much less understand) at first but later realized they were the absolute best for me because they came from His hand. He's good to me that way.

"In everything
give thanks:
for this is God's will for you
in Christ Jesus. "[xiv]

Life and Death

I woke up one Sunday morning with a sharp pain in my chest, and great difficulty getting anything more than a very shallow breath. Yes, I know, those could be heart attack symptoms, but I didn't think that was what it was and didn't want to go to an ER.

Because I am not a doctor, and my husband thought that we might need to see one. Slight understatement. I relented and made an appointment with our family doctor on Monday. He determined I needed to be hospitalized. He wouldn't look me in the eye, but said out loud that he thought I might be in the end stage of some undiscovered cancer.

The tests revealed fluid around my heart and lungs which explained my inability to get a full breath. The fancy medical terms they used for that part of my distress were "pericardial and pleural effusions.'

Several other rather important organs were "in distress" to say the least. The blood-work suggested I was "crashing," so I was transferred to a larger hospital and into a cardiac unit.

Several specialists in addition to the cardiologist were called in, and still no one could determine the cause of all this, though all tried diligently to help me. They even speculated about the possibility of a bird virus—no offense Oscar. Several people researched, but no one found any bird virus that could be transmitted to humans with my symptoms.

By the way, a sweet friend took bird duty for me while I was away.

Many dear friends came to visit, and our pastor was there nearly every day. I realized the severity of the situation but had a great peace, the kind that surpasses all comprehension.[xv] I did not have an assurance that I would survive, but rather that I was in His hand and surrounded by His love.

Many prayers were offered on my behalf. You may recall from the eighth chapter of Revelation that the prayers of the saints are in the very throne room of God.[xvi] I am convinced that He hears every one, and I am equally convinced that His decision about the outcome is worthy of my complete and utmost trust.

I tried to comfort those who were concerned by assuring them that "anything that draws me nearer to the throne of God is a good thing." I was, and remain, so very grateful that so many have taken my name to the throne of the God of heaven.

I had the great privilege to speak with many people who came in and out of my hospital room. There were nurses who needed to hear a word of encouragement from God and who needed to see an immediate prayer answered. My veins were collapsing and blowing out, which made for great difficulty in starting IVs and gathering the constant blood samples. You can imagine their distress (and mine). After many tries, one exasperated nurse said "Cross your fingers this time.,"

I said, "I would rather pray."

That time she got the vein and it didn't blow out. She took a breath, looked up, cocked her head sideways and said "You prayed, didn't you?"

I smiled. We had a nice talk, and she left with a smile, too.

The identification tag of one employee revealed her name was Esther. We had a great conversation about being prepared and equipped for "such a time as this."[xvii] After all, I had been given the opportunity to witness how the suffering of one little hummingbird could minister to my heart. Perhaps it was my turn to be injured and to minister.[xviii]

One visitor came who shares my love for "critters." I wanted to tell him about Oscar and prayed as he came in that I would be able to share the story. I didn't get to, though, for God had already planned out something much better! Because of my difficulty breathing (and therefore talking), he told me his hummingbird story instead.

He had recently found a hummingbird completely entangled in a spider web. The bird was motionless, so he thought it was dead. He meticulously removed him from the web and began to feel the thumping of a heartbeat in his hand (sound familiar?). My heart was racing and I could hardly contain myself. Thankfully, God contained and restrained me.

His story continued. The little bird was unconscious, so he blew little puffs of his warm breath onto his tiny face. His hummer responded by opening his eyes and was rewarded with some sugar-water. He held him until he regained his faculties then placed him on a bush. After a while he flew away. (Don't you just love it?)

Finally, I could stand it no longer. "That is exactly what God wants to do! Only God can rescue you from the entanglement of sin, and only He can give you the breath of life and all that you need to be free and have life!" What an honor and blessing! I was thrilled to be given both the opportunity and the breath to share this powerful picture of God, and His desire to rescue us from our hopeless entanglement in sin!

It is true that His power is perfected in my weakness.[xix] What I could not do, He did (and with a much better plan than mine)! My heart still rejoices over the number of people God brought in and out of the room while I was there and how He allowed little ol' me to see His hand at work.

After a week in the cardiac unit, a pericardiocentesis, and lots of drugs and prayers, I was well enough to go home. Additional symptoms appeared and were added to my growing list of complications. Biopsies, tests, and consultations became part of our new normal.

∞　∞　∞

As one out-of-town consultation neared, I felt I needed to be prepared to be admitted to the hospital again and that included preparation for "bird care" while I was away.

I noticed a few mites had tagged along from their outdoor adventures and invaded Oscar and Windy's home. I let the two of them stay in the outdoor bird room while I cleaned the sand where the mites might be hiding. After I finished, I waited a while and put the birds back in.

When I came back to check on them an hour or so later, they were both motionless on the sandy floor of their home. Surely, they were just having a reaction to some remaining cleaner fumes in the sand. I lifted them out of the sand and tried desperately to revive them. I blew quick breaths of air onto their little faces, called out their names and jostled them in my hand (the best bird CPR I could muster). There was no reaction. By now tears were clouding my vision and my head spun. I simply could not believe it!

Hopefulness and reality wrestled in my mind as minutes went by and their bodies remained lifeless in my hand. No thumping heartbeat from either Oscar or Windy against my palm. The horrible truth was too much to comprehend, so I kept trying, praying and hoping. How could it be that I had taken the lives of the birds I tried so hard to help live? Yet, they were gone. DEAD!

Absolutely crushed, I returned inside with my heart in my throat and my sweet little birds in my hand, I opened my hands to show my husband what I could hardly make my mouth say out loud.

My tragic mistake that seemed like such a good idea, cost them their lives. Unknowingly, what I considered "clean" was evidently toxic to them and now it was too late to undo the wrong.

Using the consequence of my mistake, God taught me that day in a very personal way that "there is a way which seems right to man", but the end result of what we think to be right actually leads to destruction and death.[xx]

It wasn't a problem that I tried to do a good thing. The problem came when I didn't take the time to call the rehabber I worked under for instructions. I thought I knew what I was doing, but didn't. I cost these birds their lives.

Likewise, I often have what I consider to be perfectly good ideas about how things should be handled. My ideas aren't always in God's plan. When I put them into action without asking His permission or guidance, I usually mess things up.

I have learned God doesn't need my plans to accomplish His will. Maybe you have experienced that too.

Another lesson here is that some of us try to do good things, try to do the right thing in the hope that over the course of our lives we do more good things than bad. There is a popular belief that God will weigh a balance to decide if our good outweighs our bad and we can enter into heaven based upon our good deeds.

That may seem logical humanly speaking, but please understand that the result of sin is separation from God[xxi] and no entrance into heaven. Any sin, in thought or deed, disqualifies me. The only hope I have for entrance, is being cleansed by and covered in His righteousness.[xxii]

As Oscar delighted in his rain shower clean-up, I rejoice in my clean-up that only God can provide. I need Him and His righteousness to make me the kind of clean required to enter the gates of heaven.[xxiii]Oscar and Windy needed me for their lives, and I tried my very best but, that human effort failed. We need God, and unlike humans, He will never fail us.[xxiv] His ways are always perfect, in timing and in substance.

I am much more likely now than ever before, to pray before I act.

Blessings in Brokenness

It has now been six years since I first "got sick." I have had multiple surgeries and still no human answers as to why this is happening in my body. I have limitations in my ability to do many of the things that I formerly took for granted, such as driving, walking, and using my hands.

I now use a cane (though I prefer to call it "my stick") when walking in public and have found it to be quite a blessing. It is a blessing to remain steady instead of wobbly, and a blessing to have opportunities to share with people who are kind enough to ask about my walking problem. God has provided a built-in audience and has given me many opportunities to share the grace, mercy and sufficiency of God. What an absolute blessing, indeed, that He has given to me!

My many doctor visits have put me in the company of those who need to hear about the love of God in waiting rooms, offices, and operating rooms. What a wonderful blessing of opportunity, not to mention captive audience! So, although the doctors do not know why this is happening to me, God does. Isn't it just beautiful? He is using me in my brokenness. He has put me directly where He wants to use me, in the path of the hurting, just as He taught me with Oscar.

Though many have prayed for my complete physical healing, and God is certainly completely able to fulfill that request, He has chosen for my body to remain unhealed. I have great joy in reminding people that I have been healed of my greatest sickness, my sin sickness. That, my friends, is the sickness that leads to eternal death.[xxv] From that sickness I have been completely healed!

If I were physically healthy, I would still be working. Instead, I have given up paying jobs and even volunteer jobs that I am no longer equipped to do. The one remaining job I can accomplish isn't a paying job in the usual sense. I lead an in-depth Bible study one day per week. There is no monetary paycheck but, I am being filled with things of far greater value.[xxvi]

What a blessing I would be missing if I were not broken! You see, He fully equipped[xxvii] me for where He needed me to be and has sufficiently supplied the grace[xxviii] I need to deal with this "momentary, light affliction"[xxix] and to honor and glorify Him through it all. He stripped me of what I thought were my strengths and made me weak in order to demonstrate His strength. He even used a broken little bird to show me.

God used these sufferings of life to teach me about real beauty, Himself, and His love for me. Had Oscar not suffered his "bad day," I might never have witnessed the majestic beauty of God's hummingbird handiwork so closely and personally. I might never have put to life the words He taught about His care for birds, and His even greater measure of care for me. What a blessing for me out of the hardship of a bird!

When Job suffered the loss of possessions, health, and family, when Daniel was taken away from his home into captivity and spent a night with lions, when Joseph was sold by his brothers into slavery in a foreign country, and when Oscar was attacked, do you think they asked for these hardships and misfortunes to befall them?

I doubt it.

Did God cause it to work together for good?[xxx]

Of this I have no doubt.

Through Oscar, I saw myself as God sees me, beautiful in my brokenness, and that makes me truly blessed beyond measure!

For you I pray the same things that I pray for myself; that the hand of God will be evident to you in good times and in bad. I pray that you will not only

recognize His hand, but also

find rest and peace there and that

you will be willing to hold onto that hand and

walk with Him wherever He wants you to go, and

be exactly who He created you to be.

Lasting Lessons I Learned from Oscar

- ❖ Curiosity might have killed the cat, but it could also lead you to see a miracle you might have missed otherwise.
- ❖ Don't be afraid to offer help to someone who needs it.
- ❖ Don't be afraid to ask for and accept help when you need it.
- ❖ When your head is wobbly and you are confused, look to Him.
- ❖ God will equip you with what you need and teach you how to accomplish the task He gives to you.
- ❖ Don't give up hope. It may seem like you are left alone, but God can orchestrate a rescue in a way you least expect it.
- ❖ God cares for the tiniest birds of the air and He loves you far more than any of them.
- ❖ You are beautiful in His sight.
- ❖ Your character and behavior will define how you are known, regardless of your given name.
- ❖ Rejoice in the little things. Even when life is hard, it helps to sing in the shower.
- ❖ God wants to spend time with you in the garden.
- ❖ Bitterness robs you of the joy of today. Forgiveness is better.
- ❖ Demanding that God do everything your way is foolish. He already wants to give you the very best.
- ❖ Good deeds are not good enough.
- ❖ Pain and suffering are a part of life.
- ❖ Brokenness and blessing can come hand in hand.
- ❖ If it brings you closer to Him, it is good.

Life in the Pond

Big Daddy

He was quite the bully from the very start. First in line for food, he always took more than his share. This tyrant even had the nerve to go right up to the other fishes' faces and try to suck the food right out of their mouths. He learned that it would intimidate them into choking up some crumbs from their bite, thus leaving scraps for him. Sometimes he would browbeat them into releasing the whole bite!

Think he knows he is handsome?

Some were shy, and stayed back until the coast was clear. Then when everyone was busy chewing, then they came in for leftovers. These timid ones were perpetually small, and "you know who" grew larger. I never knew that goldfish had such individual personalities and was thoroughly entertained to sit alongside the edge of the pond just watching and discovering who they were. Names were gradually assigned according to their behavior. Thus, the self-nominated dictator of a goldfish who "ruled the roost" came to be known as Big Daddy of the pond.

Our first "crop" of a dozen goldfish who all looked so similar (think "little patches of wiggling glitter") when they were an inch to an inch-and-a-half long in a little pet store aquarium, now were becoming little three to four-inch individual characters in their very own outdoor pond. Each is beautiful in his or her own way.

Blue Girl has pale white skin and scales with blue eyelids. She was sick during her first winter and was found floating on her side many times. I would talk to her, nudge her, gently stroke her side or belly, place food by her mouth and put dissolvable tablets, designed for sick aquarium fish, near her. She struggled for months, or at least convinced me she was struggling, and I continued to pamper and encourage her.

Now, five years later, at feeding time she still occasionally comes to the edge of the pond and jumps up onto a flat rock half out of the water to beg for food, and belly rubs.

Feeding time at our little pond produces a stampede of spoiled little fish. I like to call it "roll call." When I show up at the water's edge with their food, their slow motion, graceful, gliding suddenly transforms to a wild rush of splashing water, pleading eyes, and tiny fish lips that come up out of the water and crowd together to get as close

as possible to the hand that feeds them.

My diva, Blue Girl, half out of the water waiting for a belly rub.

They assemble in a glittery glob in front of me, pantomiming "more, more, more." (Go to a mirror and try it, you will see what I mean. I won't tell.) They all receive a generous feeding allowance, but Blue Girl gets the talent award.

Little Goldie is a shy girl with a blonde face who waits her turn at the back of the feeding line. She remains small, even though I always find her in the crowd and toss some pellets her way.

Flipper is a silly little comedian who does a good dolphin imitation. I don't know if he is just hyperactive or if he has a fish phobia (complex?) and leaps out of the water away from imaginary sharks. Maybe he is just training for the fish Olympics, but he's not saying.

Rocky found himself trapped between a rock and a hard place. By the time he was rescued he had scraped some of his orange scales off his face. His white spot on his cute little orange face makes him easy to recognize.

Stub is a plain and portly girl with balance issues; she lists to the side just a bit.

Valentino is a son of Big Daddy. He is a glorious dark red, has his father's beautiful fantail, and is a real ladies man—uhm—fish.

Adventures

E ven in Alabama, winters sometimes cause several inches of ice to form over our pond. We worried about our little finned friends that first harsh winter, but they knew to swim slowly, save energy, and wait for spring. We were amazed to see them deep under the ice, moving slowly, but moving.

We have only lost one fish. Poor little guy, he learned the hard way that you should never kiss the pump. We found him one morning during a morning roll call, but it was too late to save him.

My sweet little Blue Girl also had a close call that first spring. When the water warms up, it is time for big fishes to make little fishes. The mommy fish develop eggs, and the daddy fish nudge (chase, pester, bump, shove, prod…whatever it takes) the mommy fish until the mommy fish release their eggs. The daddy fish all follow her and try to fertilize the eggs as she releases them. Sometimes the chase goes on for weeks. (In case you were wondering, this observation also led to some clarity with their names.)

During her first "spring chase" with us, Blue Girl became hopelessly caught in some netting that was tightly wound around the root of a water lily. She was completely wedged up into the net against the root ball of the plant and could no longer move anything but her one of her gills. I tried, but wasn't able to untangle her by hand, and had to bring out some scissors to cut her loose from the netting.

It must have seemed like a good idea to her at the time to lay eggs in the safety of the roots, but she obviously didn't anticipate the entanglement that could have cost her life. But lay many eggs, she did, and she now has a lovely look-alike daughter with blue eye lids.

Our first dozen fish increased the herd then and every year since. Many have a strong resemblance to Big Daddy who is now about ten inches long with a spectacular three-inch or more fantail. He is the standout among the other more ordinary six to eight-inch fish. When people see our little fish collection for the first time, he is the one most likely to get the "Ohhs" and "Ahhs." He still tries to be first in line for everything, including the spring chase.

At this writing, it is spring, and as usual, the chase is on. This spring though, Big Daddy was suddenly and for the first time, absent from morning roll call and feeding. We looked under all the plants (remembering Blue Girl's predicament we had already removed all the netting from the water plants). We considered several possibilities.

Maybe he took on a snake that was bigger than he was. The predator could have been a patient cat, but we found no remains. Maybe a falcon or hawk took him out for lunch. The other fish weren't talking, but we didn't really have any evidence of a conspiracy on their part. Poor Big Daddy. The pond just wasn't the same without him.

After three days of mourning, guess who showed up for feeding time? He was thinner, scarred, and barely moving. Several of his beautiful, sparkling, golden scales were missing, leaving him with bare white patches. A few remaining scales were just barely holding on. One fin was almost useless, and with it not working properly, he struggled to not swim in circles. He was back, but he was not quite his splendid former self.

Unless the snake spit the bully back out, the cat didn't savor the golden swimmer and returned him, or the hawk had all the bullying he could take, Big Daddy must have gotten himself wedged between some rocks, had to suffer the consequences, and let the others be first in line for a few days until he lost a little weight in order to free himself.

His fins and scales have since healed, although some previously gold scales are now white. Like an old fish, he seems slower and grayer, and not always up for a showdown. Now he isn't always first for feeding, but he does seem grateful just to swim with the herd. To me he will long be the Big Daddy of the bunch, maybe even better now with a good dose of humility.

Lisa Worthey Smith

Truths for Us
From the Pond

- ❖ The fish didn't choose their pond. They were placed there by the pond owner.

- ❖ Fish are beautiful to their pond owner.

- ❖ Their behavior tells the world who they are.

- ❖ Beauty is fleeting. Wisdom is better.

- ❖ The pond owner gives them what they need, daily.

- ❖ The fish can never loose themselves from their entanglement, only the pond owner can cut them loose.

- ❖ When winter is hard, keep swimming.

- ❖ Each fish has to individually face consequences of his own behavior.

- ❖ Sometimes those consequences leave scars that will be recognized by those around them.

- ❖ The command to be fruitful still stands.

❖ Hormones and feelings can lead fish to make bad choices with dire results.

❖ Winter comes. Keep swimming. Spring will come after even the hardest winter. (Yes, I know this has already been listed, but winter comes every year!)

❖ Those with humility are rewarded by the pond owner.

❖ Bullies eventually get their due dose of humility.

❖ Family resemblance is based on both appearance and behavior.

❖ The pond owner is always nearby.

Likewise:

- ❖ God is the good pond owner Who put us in the place He chose for us.

- ❖ He knows and loves us. We are beautiful in His sight.

- ❖ Our behavior tells the world who we are.

- ❖ Beauty is fleeting. Wisdom is better.

- ❖ God knows our needs and is able to supply all our needs.

- ❖ We can never free ourselves from our sin entanglement. Only God can free us.

- ❖ Life can be hard. Keep going.

- ❖ He allows us to make mistakes, and suffer the consequences.

- ❖ Those consequences can have long term scars that will be recognized by others.

- ❖ The command to be "fruitful" still stands. We need to make more disciples.

- ❖ Hormones and feelings can lead us to make bad choices with dire results.

- ❖ Hard times will come. Keep swimming, and remember that winter is just a season. Spring will come.

- ❖ Jesus was humble and expects us to be the same. Humility will be rewarded.

- ❖ Bullies will reap what they sow.

- ❖ We should behave like our Father.

- ❖ God is always nearby.

Life in the Garden

Daylilies

S ome people absolutely seem to have a green thumb. Both of my grandmothers could cut a piece of a plant, put it in a little cup of water or in the ground, explain to the cutting what it should do, and it would grow in sheer obedience to their command. That's a green thumb.

I often have little jars with baby plants and sweet talk them with my best green thumb voice. Some make it, some don't. So rather than a green thumb, I have a brown one. I dig and plant until somebody wants to grow. If they don't seem to like location, I dig them up again and move them to a new locale. My husband likes to tell people that when plants go to sleep in the fall, they don't know where they will wake up in the spring.

Daylilies are some of my favorites, and we have hundreds in our backyard; early bloomers, late bloomers, singles, doubles, triples, tall, short, buttery yellow, light red, dark red, bronze, and many, many in between.

The early bloomers usually begin their dazzling exhibit the first week in June. The buttery-yellow show offs came from my husband's grandmother who lived in Tampa, Florida. Early in our married life I was given a handful of these garden jewels and they have multiplied and bloomed every year since. That started a "fever," if you will. They have always been so easy to please. Simply plant them in a sunny spot and watch them grow.

As other larger trees and bushes matured, I had to separate and relocate them to sunnier places in the yard, thus Mr. Tall, Dark & Handsome's running joke. Truth is, I am fascinated by planting seeds, cuttings, and roots and watching them grow. The worms and ladybugs just add to the fun. Some say I am easily entertained. Well, bless their little hearts. They are just missing out on the fun life!

These wonderful daylilies now grace our yard with glorious blooms that unfortunately only last - you guessed it - a single day. So, that warrants a trip through the garden every day to see who is blooming that day.

A garden owner enjoys the beauty of the garden but is also required to be a garden tender. The health of the garden will reflect the diligence of the gardener. A good daylily gardener will dead-head (remove) the spent blooms each day. In recent years, I have not been able to tend to the garden as I did before, and because of my neglect some blooms were unable to open. When I didn't dead-head, the spent flowers from Monday withered and became encrusted onto the buds of flowers yet to bloom.

When Wednesday's bloom tried to open, it was strangled by the withered blooms and could not release itself from their entrapment. It could have been splendid, but the best it could do was to swell out a bit. What a shame. What could have been a day of glorious blooming, lost.

Strangled bloomers.

Have you ever felt like that? As if strangled by something outside your control? Life events, family, health, finances all can leave us with heavy burdens that

68

can be so overwhelming they seem to limit, even crush, our lives.

I try to remember that each day has both responsibilities and opportunities that are only available that one day. No matter the circumstance that looms heavily around me, I still have that responsibility and opportunity and don't want to miss it using something or someone else as my excuse.

Even the strongest of us can't overcome everything on our own. I'm so very, very thankful for the Master Gardener Who has planted me, watered me, and given me everything I need to thrive. I know without a doubt that He will never leave a circumstance over me that He cannot remove, or that He cannot give me strength enough to overcome in order to bloom that day.[xxxi] I desire nothing more than His hand tending to me in order that I will somehow be a bloom, however briefly, for Him.

Law of the Harvest

You have probably noticed that if you plant okra, okra will grow. Nice how that works, isn't it? Now, don't get me wrong, I have mistaken Jalapeno seeds for sweet bell pepper seeds and been quite surprised at the little guys that were produced! But that was my fault, not the seed's fault. The seed knew exactly what it was and produced accordingly. I didn't label the seeds and planted the wrong ones.

Okra

Never have I planted an okra seed and had corn or radishes come up. It's a rule, a "law" if you will. It is sometimes referred to as the "law of the harvest." The harvest will be exactly what was planted.

Seeds are like that. They do what they are supposed to do. Likewise, if we plant seeds of hatred, they will grow. Love, respect, and kindness sprout when and where they are sown, too.

Be careful what you sow.

If we consider ourselves seeds which were planted by God, then we might be guilty of being tempted to try to do or be something we are not. How foolish would it be for a person to try to be a house? It won't work, I promise.

You are not designed or equipped to be a house. You are uniquely designed and equipped to be YOU! God made no mistake in creating you, just as you are. He planted you in a particular place and will nurture you to be the person you were created to be. My friend, if that doesn't make you smile, then … well, you just need to read it again!

You are perfectly designed, created, and planted by the Master of the Universe. Whew! What a relief! I admit that it is tempting to compare ourselves to the okra planted next to us with their pretty little blooms, or the corn on the next row with tall sturdy stalks and silken tops. But, try to remember that God only expects you to be the person He created.

Every garden has variety, and His is no different. He doesn't expect you to be a squash if He made you a turnip. Just grow and trust Him to use you. He has just the right plans for you.

Find out what they are and flourish.

Bloom
Where You Are Planted

Hostas are among those charming plants which thrive in the shade or with filtered sunlight. My beautiful broad-leafed, variegated hostas live the life of luxury beneath two mature Sugar Maple trees.

In the heat of the summer, they are cooled by the shade of these stately forty-foot tall beauties. They allow little dappled splotches (maybe a horticultural term: spots + patches?) of precious sunlight to dance over the underlying ground. It is lovely to behold. I call them "light freckles." With every passing southern breeze they glide over the plants, giving them just enough of a sunshine tickle to grow without blasting them with so much it burns their tender foliage. In return, the hostas provide additional shade and moisture for the roots of the maples. Isn't it nice when neighbors get along?

On the other hand, the fig trees have need of full sun. They are among those of which Mr. Tall, Dark & Handsome speaks. They are now in their third location in the yard, pending another possible move. I just haven't found the right spot.

I thought they would need a little protection from the afternoon sun, so their initial location was about twenty feet from a tree line that offered late afternoon shade. It didn't work; too much shade and competition for moisture from outlying roots of those shade-giving trees.

So, location number two landed it another ten feet away from the tree line, but still too much shade and root competition. Now in location number three, we finally have a few figs, but the verdict isn't final. If the trees soak every drop of moisture and don't leave enough for the figs, they may have to pack their bags again.

My trial and error method should give you a clue that I am not a Master Gardener. I keep trying and learning but still make mistakes. My poor little plants understand the shuffle routine and try their best to cooperate but they probably cringe when I reach for the shovel, or send Mr. T D & H their way.

Some new additions to our yard this year are grape vines. Well, they aren't exactly vines yet. They started as carefully pruned cuttings from a friend who has cultivated, researched, and grown grapes for years. He graciously shared the cuttings and some expert advice on planting.

For quite some time after the cuttings arrived, they were just sticks in the mud—literally. I am quite sure they will do their part and try to grow, but time will tell whether or not I did my part well and chose a proper location and provided proper care. If I did, there will be grape jelly to share in a few years! If not, you know the drill—move 'em, move 'em, move 'em!

THE Master Gardener works in an altogether different manner from my trial and error system. He knows us. He knows the soil, sun and water requirements we need. He also knows who needs what you and I have to offer. Knowing all that, He will plant us in the perfect spot. That is not to say that the location won't change.

I have been moved from time to time. Sometimes it seemed like it was for my benefit, and sometimes it seemed to be more a ministry to others (each of which is a blessing). Maybe you have experienced that, too. While I thought I was in a great location each time, I was moved to a new place of ministry.

So, without excuse, we should be blooming where He has planted us—without complaining about greener grass on the other side of the fence. As Erma Bombeck noted, the grass is always greener over the septic tank! If you feel like a stick in the mud, don't worry, He has great plans for you and can make you thrive!

Filled with
His Fragrance

Do you have a favorite fragrance in the garden? Here in the South, when the farmers first till the red clay where the cotton will grow, that is one of my all-time favorites. Yes, the freshly tilled dirt. It literally draws me to inhale a little deeper. If not for trespassing, I would take off my shoes and go barefoot into the fields, and dig my toes into the warm fresh soil, and let my hands scoop up hands-full of the rich dirt, worms and all. Mmmmm, it makes my eyes roll back in

Lemon blossom

my head just thinking about it! Can you smell it?

Well, okay. I get it. It may not be your favorite smell. You might prefer roses. There is a Mr. Lincoln rose in our yard that our son helped to choose when he was just a little boy. The first rose bloom of the season usually occurs early May, just in time for Mother's Day! It has ruby-red velvety blooms on long stems and smells, well, just like a rose should smell! With its timing and beauty, the first-fruit is usually snipped and given as a gift to someone very special. It is among my favorite of the fragrances.

Then again, there are the herbs such as rosemary, sage and lemon balm. Like many herbs, they have blooms, but the leaves produce the fragrance. All it takes is a little brush against these plants for them to share their scent.

Our rosemary bush has supplied the flavoring for many herb-baked chickens, turkeys, potatoes, and loaves of bread. When I snip it, I carry with me the rosemary fragrance the rest of the day, despite numerous washings of my hands.

It is the same with a patch of lemon balm near our outdoor seating area. Once pinched, broken, and crushed, the lemony leaves release their fragrance on us, and while it lingers, it helps to discourage mosquitoes for a while. It is prolific and generous enough to replace any and all that we swipe from spring until fall. Its leaves can also be used to make a tea. Its generosity befuddles most, in that when it is crushed and boiled, it releases its fragrance. I dare say I would not react so kindly.

Speaking of lemons (sort of), a sweet and generous relative spent over a decade raising a lush and beautiful lemon tree from a seed. He graciously entrusted his baby to me. (He has unlimited visitation rights, by the way.)

It spends the winter in the sunroom. Then, when all danger of frost has passed it spends the warm months in the yard. Once outside, it takes a deep breath, and begins production of glossy dark-green leaves. Soon, blossoms emerge and attract bees from the surrounding neighborhoods. I didn't actually do a survey of the bees mind you, but I did observe many more bees than normal. I don't blame the little buzzers, it was worth the trip, I am quite sure!

The sweet and lovely fragrance has even earned a song of its very own! It is an oldie. Do you remember? "Lemon tree very pretty, and the flowers smell so sweet …" You have to admit that not many other scents have inspired a song. This one is truly a fragrance extraordinaire! When I find a way to insert a "scratch and sniff" page for you, I promise I will!

If only I could share an enormous sweet lemon.

I'll work on that, too.

While I enjoy a whiff of a passing sweet aroma, when I handle the rosemary, sage, lemon balm or blossoms, their fragrances transfer to me and I carry their aroma for the rest of the day. Mr. T D & H always notices when I have been around any of these because the fragrance lingers on me for a time. Cutting onions, burning leaves, encountering a skunk or baking cookies all leave no doubt to bystanders of our recent activity because the lingering aroma.

In a sense, when we spend time with God we carry His fragrance with us. The more time we spend with Him, the more our thoughts, words and actions become like His. When our words and actions come from Him, it is as if His fragrance oozes from us.

Beyond that, when our lives reflect Christ, we share that "sweet aroma" with those whose lives we touch. [xxxii] Now, that's a fragrance worth seeking out, handling, wearing and sharing!

Lisa Worthey Smith

My Conversation with a Cuckoo

Until that day, I had never had been formally introduced to a cuckoo—bird, that is. This meeting was not one of niceties, but of necessity.

This one made a bad decision; a really bad decision. He flew into a garage. Mind you, that in itself isn't such a bad thing—unless you don't know the way out. He didn't.

After a long while of avoiding his rescuer and trying to fly out of the ceiling and knocking down the garage door rails, he tired enough for my husband—Mr. Tall Dark & Handsome—to nab him.

Mr. T D & H presented his catch to me wrapped in a chamois, from said garage. Mr. Cuckoo was a mess. His bloodied head told me he butted against walls with all his little bird strength to find his way out.

Cuckoo burrito.

A closer inspection—much to his disliking—revealed his head feathers were broken off at the nub.

Just a guess but, he might have a stubborn streak.

Once a rehabber, always a rehabber. Rubber gloves, paper towels, water, aloe were my initial tools for this job.

We found a spot in the shade and started to work. The glaring from his eyes told me he didn't appreciate it one bit. He needed attention so, despite the death stare, I took the end of a paper towel and wet it to clean his bloody head. His protests quieted so the cool water must have been some comfort.

After a few dabs I found no lacerations, so I finished cleaning and applied a little aloe for healing. With him safely wrapped like a chamois cuckoo burrito, and turned him over. There were no other obvious wounds.

His screams of protest began again when he was upright. I can't give you an exact translation because I am not fluent in Cuckoo. I can tell you if Mommy Cuckoo was listening, he may be in for a "washing of the beak!"

We found him well enough to try for a release. His patience with me obviously coming to an end, I took a picture. Notice his "sweet smile?" Stubborn and unhappy.

We no more than unwrapped his burrito than off he flew.

No thank you.

No tender good-byes.

Off to the nearest tree and life as before. He may have some explaining to do about his head injury but he should be fine.

If the guy had used a helmet he could have avoided his injury. I am sorry he had such a rough day. Because he didn't listen when Mr. TD&H tried to explain the way out for him, he probably wouldn't have listened to me either. We did what we could in light of his situation. It is up to him whether or not he learned any lessons.

The same is true for us. The *helmet of salvation* protects us from injury to our heads. Indeed, our enemy wants to get in there and bloody us up with false teachings. He is the father of lies and will do his best to fill our heads with them—unless we have our helmet.

Things I learned

- Without God, we are likely to go places and be found in situations that cause us harm and from which we can't find our way out.
- When (Christian) help comes, it would be beneficial to listen.
- When offering help (Truth) to one in distress, you may encounter screams of protest. Be willing to wait and offer Truth anyway. Earnestly contend for the faith.
- When offering Truth, you must be prepared for both reception and rejection. Offer Truth anyway.
- When you give life-saving Truth to one and they reject it today, it may open a door to another day. Don't be discouraged – one plants, another waters – God gives the increase.
- If you reject the Truth, you can expect to make harmful decisions over and over again.

Cuckoos are considered "brood parasites." They often lay their eggs in another's nest. If you find a cuckoo in your nest,

- Take care of them as if they are your own.
- Teach them the Truth.
- Give them access to a helmet.
- Realize – the decision is theirs.

Cuckoo with his catch

Things Change

It is true. Things change. What was perfectly happy to be planted near the pond last year may be overshadowed by the penny-wort the next year, and begging to have its own space. That's my job - not so much to keep everybody happy, but to have them in their proper places.

Indeed, our garden sometimes seems to be in constant motion. As the Sugar Maples matured and spread out ever wider, (No. I won't go there) the lilies that were happy alongside them had to be moved out from under their now shady limbs to a sunnier spot. They do love their sunshine.

Then there were the lush and beautiful hostas that were so happy that they multiplied. The problem was that when they multiplied, they grew on top of each other to the point of crowding each other out of house and home, or dirt and sun in this case.

Now, left alone, they would die of mutual suffocation.

The remedy? Dig them up, separate, share with a friend, and replant

Garlic Chives

the extras in a new bed, so they can all live, grow, and multiply some more. Thus, our garden expands and is ever-changing.

A number of years ago I bought a four-inch pot of garlic chives. They are dandy little guys for sprucing up omelets, roasted potatoes, spaghetti, butter for bread, and lots of other tasty opportunities. Dandy little guys indeed, the first year, that is.

As they matured that first season, they shot up seed pods that drooped over a few inches and deposited seeds for next year. Well, that was fine, but now several years later, the whole neighborhood has garlic chives. We could share chives with the whole county!

Some plants are so prolific and produce so many offspring, that if left in one place, the garden would be overflowing with them. So, their seeds need to be gathered and shared or planted in pots to share in the spring.

It seems to me that God works in a similar way with us. Some are prolific producers and generations from now their offspring will still be sowing seeds. But just when we think we are in a happy spot, we get moved away from our comfort zone, placed in a new place with a new group and new set of opportunities. While it may not be our choice, it certainly is for our good. He trims us and divides us sometimes to help us have room to grow, and sometimes to let us start a new "clump." Sometimes we may not even recognize why our world is torn upside down.

Whether or not my lilies know why I dig them up, separate them from their friends, and put them in another place, or my chives understand why I gather their precious little seeds, I will do my best to take care of them.

How much more we can always trust the Master Gardener to place us exactly where He knows we need to be.

The Slightly Disobedient Frog

There once was a young little frog,
  Who liked to play in the bog,
So he stayed and he played,
Long after they said,
He should "leave for the day and go home".

He knew what was best, he thought,
And said to himself, "I'm quite smart,
So, I'll do as I please,
I'm tired of their pleas,
To stop having fun and get out."

So, he splashed a bit more in the pond,
And swam with the fishes 'til dawn.
He had heard all the warnings,
But still stayed until morning,
Romping with high froggie fun.

The Slightly Disobedient Frog

He only thought he was quite bright,
And stayed much long that night.
Then when the temperature plunged,
And he no longer could jump,
It cost him the rest of his life.

Just a slightly disobedient frog
Having oh, so much fun in the bog,

He only wanted to play,
More than obey
The wisdom of those on the log.

So our tale starts again with us two,
Yes, that's me and perhaps even you,
When we think we know better
Than God's truth in His letter
Like the frog, we lose our lives too.

The sin in our lives works that way.
"Just stay a bit longer and play"
Is the song that it sings
While it lies and deceives
Us more and more every day.

Venturing outside of His will,
Looking for all the cheap thrills,
We stay far too long,
Blinded by wrong,
Until we lose both our lives and the thrill.

So, now comes the time for our test,
When we try to determine what's best,
Listen to wisdom? Obey?
Or be happy to stay and just play?
Seems clear to me, want to guess?

The sad, little tale of the frog,
Does not have to be yours at all!

You can trust God today,
Have life, and obey,

And live happily in the grandest way of all!

The Life and Times of Miss Polly

S he is as prettty as they come, don't you think?

The proper name of this grand plump caterpillar is Anamalia Arthropoda Insecta Lepidoptera Papilionidae Papilionini Papilio P. polyxenes.

Miss Polly
ready for a change.

I call her Miss Polly. You may too, if you like.

Her story began right here in my back yard, on a nice stand of fragrant heirloom dill. She doesn't know I planted it just for her but, that's okay.

It was a warm day in June—aren't they all—when her mother laid her there. After about a week of being a baby, she "hatched" into a tiny, black larvae—her childhood.

I first noticed Miss Polly when she entered her young adult time as a caterpillar. She was bright yellow/green with luxurious black stripes that accentuated her curves in all the right places. Her numerous—although stubby—legs were just right for holding a fancy little caterpillar onto a dill stem.

I marvelled for a good two weeks at her beauty and voracious appetite. Then, just as God designed, the time came for her to leave her brothers and sisters, and she knew it.

Her itty-bitty legs took her all the way down the dill to a new place, somewhere she had never been before. She found a good sturdy stick from a neighboring daylily and bravely climbed into this new territory.

After she had the lasso in just the right spot, the time came to surrender to the inevitable. She was leaving her caterpillar life. No more munching on tender dill strands with her family. That part of her life was over.

In faith, she released her legs from the stem and allowed the lasso hold her. Her faith was rewarded. Now it was time for the transition to begin.

July 19, she set herself on the stick. The next morning, she was encased in this chrysalis of a casket. Her earth-bound caterpillar life was behind her.

Nine days later she emerged from her temporary casket. No longer a pudgy caterpillar, she emerged a lovely long-legged beauty with glorious wings!

It only took her about an hour to dry out her brand-new wings, say goodbye, and take flight. She is still the same little girl of a caterpillar that I visited over the course of her lifetime yet, she is now different!

That part of her life, limited to crawling less than three feet off the ground, is over! She has a new life, with wings to fly her wherever her little heart desires!

I seriously doubt that Miss Polly's caterpillar friends are grieving over her. They are probably rejoicing at her new life; full, free, and glorious!

I have several decades under my belt, and have watched the process over and over. Maybe you have too. We are born. We grow. We change. We <u>all</u> change.

My friend, we are all destined to leave this earth. Whether we die before Christ comes or we are changed when He comes, the time will come for each of us to let go of this part of our lives and be changed into an eternal state. In 1 Corinthians 15 you can learn more.

The question is where do we go from here? What happens next?

As a Christian (one who has placed full trust and faith in Christ Jesus as Savior) my next life, the eternal one, will be with Him. I have given Him my life and have trusted Him with the details of how it will play out. Meanwhile, I will do my very best to be obedient to Him while I am still here. When He decides the time has come for me to begin my new/eternal life, He will prepare and eqip me for the transition. Any casket will be temporary. My new body will be glorified yet, still me.

Those who have not accepted Jesus the Christ as their personal Savior will also wake up to an eternal life. Theirs will be one of everlasting torment. Read more about the contrast between the next life of those who do trust Him and those who not trust Him in Mark 9, Revelation 21, and 2 Thessalonians.

Truths you and I can see from Miss Polly;

- We are alive now.
- This life is temporary.
- God determines our days.
- God designed and equips me for every stage.
- This body will be left behind and we will be changed (while still ourselves.)
- The next part of our life is eternal.
- I can trust God with my today and my eternity. You can too.

Predators Will Come

If you have done any gardening whatsoever, you have probably dealt with pests. Many of them are wolves in sheep's clothing. Well, they may not be exactly wolves or sheep, but still predators in disguise nonetheless.

The horned worms which make an annual appearance on our tomato vines are a great example. The horn is not a cute little antler, but rather a giant, curved, thorn-like, weapon. A first-hand account from a friend's unfortunate encounter with one informed me that the evil-looking stinger is a pain-inflicting, effective defense.

These fat green worms are clothed in "tomato vine green" camouflage. They look so much like the tomato stems they are very difficult to notice until their damage or defense system becomes evident.

I first noticed their—uhm—poop on some leaves which prompted the manhunt, wolf tracking, bug patrol, well, actually it was a worm hunt.

I followed a short trail of destruction and found not one, but two of the chubby little green "wolves" today. From their size (at least the size of my pointer finger), they didn't just fall off the turnip truck

Horn Worm

yesterday. I obviously had been overlooking their presence for some time.

Wolves in sheep clothing indeed.

Some trespassers are a little less disguised and

slightly more obvious. It is easier to deliver a swift punishment to those. Today it was a five-footer.

My husband did the dirty deed.

A post mortem indicated he was a rat snake. I know all the "good snake" protests, so don't waste your time. I don't like them. God put enmity between us. I would like to give my frogs, birds and lizards the peace of mind that comes from living in a safe yard. If they would just sneak in at night and eat the moles and leave, the serpents could keep their little heads.

You may have encountered people who are obviously predators. They are out to take something that is yours, to "steal, kill, and destroy."[xxxiii]Some may be in disguise and thus be pretending to be something they are not. By all appearances, they are just part of the stem. Then, quietly, they devour all the tender foliage. Unchecked, they eat, grow, destroy, and multiply. They show up in our families, our circle of friends, and our churches.

Particularly dangerous are those predators who distort the truth, the Word of God, and try to make it something it is not. To know the truth, you have to read the truth, the whole truth. Taking a verse out of context is not building sound doctrine but, rather, very dangerous doctrine.

Our responsibility is to look at the whole counsel of God (read the Bible), and let Scripture interpret Scripture, rather than count on what someone believes that God thinks about a subject. That may be his or her opinion, but if it doesn't line up with Scripture, look for the "poop."

When you see the damage to God's Holy Word, you will know you are dealing with a predator. Don't turn your back, but beware, they are armed, but so are you. Use the most powerful weapon you have—THE truth. THE Word of God.

There are no "versions of the truth." Truth is truth all the time. When we treasure up (fill) our hearts with His word, the enemy may come seeking to nibble away at us, but we will be able to recognize him, and the distortion of the truth, and we will not sin against God.[xxxiv]

Don't forget to spread the wolf repellent (Scripture) all around you, your home, and your family. A fun way to immerse your home in Scripture is to tune in to a Christian radio station and sing along with Biblical truths! Not only will it lift your spirits, it will reinforce truth, and it will repel the enemy. I like to call Christian music "DDT"— Devil Deflector Tunes! It is an excellent "pest control."

Butterfly Promises

Near the end of a long and extremely cold winter, I found a brown capsule of hope—a butterfly chrysalis.

We enjoy having butterflies in our north Alabama back yard. I entice them with parsley, dill, buddleia (butterfly bush), pickerel reed, salvia, and all things blooming. In return, they entertain us with their

beauty as they flit and flutter around digging in to all the bloomers.

At times we are most handsomely rewarded with one alighting on us, but usually I am content to admire them from a respectful distance. Their incredibly lovely wings are unimaginably delicate, yet are still used as their traveling shoes—arms— wings.

Their favorite meals include the afore mentioned dill. I also like dill, and was a bit annoyed to find the little black spots on "my" plants until I saw them a few day later and they were moving.

I jumped into action.

In all honesty, I didn't *jump* but, I did investigate. When the findings were in, and I saw that the specks would end up as butterflies, I jumped for joy!

Actually, I didn't *jump*, but I did change my course of action. Instead of exterminating, I chose facilitating. I planted more dill and their second favorite, parsley. They flourished and we had cheap entertainment all summer!

Their life cycle involves the eggs being laid on some delicious foliage, then as they hatch, they devour the delicious foliage and grow into the most lovely, fat, green, segmented, worms. Well, actually, larvae.

They eat and grow to their little heart's delight until the appointed day arrives. The day of rest. All their preparatory eating would enable them to endure this next part. The rest. Miraculously (it has to be a God thing) they know to crawl up and attach themselves to something sturdy, and form into this chrysalis.

This period of rest and transformation varies with species and season. This particular chrysalis was found after months of harsh, record-breaking cold. There had been no butterfly sightings in months, and the outer part of the pod looked suspiciously dark. I commented to my husband that it either didn't survive the winter or was about to hatch.

With the possibility in mind that it might hatch at any time, I kept a close vigil. At least once a day I checked on the little guy, hopeful.

My reward came one night. The freshly hatched beauty appeared and I welcomed him into this new phase of his life. Eager to document the arrival, I took several pictures hoping the flash didn't startle him. He didn't seem to mind.

I marveled that such a small creature could survive the winter that we all grumbled about while huddling around our heaters. We had food and shelter and griped about it while he silently sat outside, alone for months, trusting that God knew what He was doing. It would be okay. Just wait.

Winter comes every year, but life is somewhat unpredictable. We know to plan for the cold, but how do we plan for life? What do we do when it seems we are abandoned in the turmoil?

Here are some great promises onto which believers in Christ can hold from James 1 and 4.

- *Count it all joy.* God reminds us that our various trials are for our good. He is always there with us, and will only allow what is good for us. Note that I didn't say what we like but, what is for our good.
- *Tests of our faith produces endurance.* If we are to finish the race (life) set before us, we need perseverance. In order to learn how to persevere we have to practice it and, build it up like a muscle to make it strong.
- *When we don't know what to do, ask God.* Knowledge can be found everywhere. Everywhere there are opinions, surveys, and theories about how you can do or resolve one thing or another. The only source for true wisdom however, is from God. He is our first and best resource. (If an opinion disagrees with His word, that is a faulty opinion.) *Note: Listen to the voice of experience - griping doesn't help.*
- *Blessings await those who persevere under trials.* (Hint – it is worn on your head). Even though the winter was long and hard, spring came.
- *Life is but a vapor and you will leave your shell.* Use this time to grow into something far more beautiful than you were. When we accept Christ, we walk in newness of life, leaving behind our "old flesh." This new walk will be with incredibly beautiful wings – Christ living in us!

When it Rains, Drink

It may seem like it would be a natural thing to do, but that is because we are the bystanders. When the rain pours down on me, it usually seems more prudent to get out of the rain. Funny how that works, especially when we are growing up. It can be hard to understand why our parents restrict us from doing the things we want to do and make us do things we do not want to do. When we are young it just seems like bullying. As we grow into a little wisdom, we realize that we learned from both being restricted and being forced to do things that were not so fun.

I don't know of any infant who liked their immunizations shots. Most scream, at least mine did. His little eyes pleaded with me to rescue him from the stinging pain of the needle, but I did not. At the time, to him, it just seemed like pain. I had no means by which I could explain to my infant son that the little bit of short-term pain would equip him to fend off dangerous assaults against him later. It was for his good in the future but hurt in the present.

Similarly, when we experience rainy seasons of pain, suffering, loneliness, injustice, or want, we can rest assured that our Father is not inflicting pain on us for no reason. Rather, He is preparing us for the future. He is strengthening us for life. He is, in a sense, allowing the rain upon us to help us grow.

How then should we respond to difficulties? It might surprise you to know that we are expected to "consider it all joy."

Why?

The "testing of your faith produces endurance."[xxxv] Before a drug is approved for public use, what happens?

It is tested.

Before you are allowed to drive alone, what happens?

You are tested.

Which recipes do you fall back upon?

The ones that have been, well, you get it.

When we become mature enough to recognize that our hard times help us rely upon our faith, they will cause our faith to grow. Then those rainy times become "more precious than gold" because they "result in praise and glory and honor" to Christ!

Our faith in Him becomes real even though we have not seen Him, "and though you do not see Him now, but believe in Him, you greatly rejoice with joy inexpressible"![xxxvi] My friend, when God sends you rain, you can know that He simply wants you to grow, so be thankful and drink!

A Little Pruning May Do You Good

Pruning is not my favorite chore in the garden. Somehow it just hurts my feelings to cut back limbs that my sweet little garden friends worked so hard to grow. I nurtured and encouraged these bloomers to grow all summer. So how could I possibly cut off that very growth? Why would I possibly be so cruel?

You guessed it - for their good. The butterfly bush, roses, Foster hollies, and various young trees all need a good trim.

Our sasanqua camellias begin their blooming season in the late fall, continuing on through January. Well, that is they bloom if they haven't had their little buds snipped off due to an untimely trim. The pruning will ideally occur just after a blooming season. If I have waited, rather, when I have waited too late, the baby buds will be trimmed off along with the straggly growth.

Timing is very important.

My timing isn't always just right, but thankfully God's is always absolutely perfect. He might trim me a bit, especially after I have bloomed, but it will be to shape me up and produce more blooms in the coming season.

For the Japanese Red Maple in our front yard, the trimming was a monthly event when it was just a first-year seedling. Looking to the future with a vision of how the tree should be shaped at maturity, I mercilessly pinched tender little twigs and leaves. It got harder and harder for me to cut the branches each year as the little tree grew stronger because the little twigs were now branches. Still, it had to be done.

If I had not snipped it while it was young, it would have grown limbs that could not have supported the mature size of the tree. Had I waited until the limbs were larger, the wounds to the sapling would be fatal. Indeed, it must be frequent, it must be done with the mature tree in mind, and it has to start early in the life of the tree. Over a period of about a decade, we had our "meetings" where I inspected and pruned.

Now years later, it has matured and our visits mostly involve my admiration of this beautiful specimen. It provides housing for little songbirds in the summer, roosting spots for Cardinals in the winter, and what must be Sunday school gathering spot for groups of Chickadees in early spring. Because it is situated just outside our dining room window, we are provided with a front row seat of the feathered visitors. It is indeed a lovely-shaped, healthy tree, a true showstopper in the front yard.

You might have been on the receiving end of the same type diligence from your parents growing up, shaping and pruning you along the way. No doubt those lessons you learned have influenced you as an adult. As a mom, "train up a child in the way he should go, even when he is old, he will not depart from it"[xxxvii] is a verse of wisdom from which I have drawn comfort for years. Our son will tell you I watched over and frequently (very frequently) snipped, corrected, and trained, him as a little sapling. Someday, he will thank me. Actually, he has. It is nice to see that God's Word remains true. How assuring that it never changes!

If it was true for the tree, and true for our son, then could it be that God uses the same technique with me? Ouch! I don't think trimming my limbs is particularly fun, but when I remember that He is looking toward the mature (eternal) result, I know I can trust Him to trim all the right places at just the right time. How I thank Him for His diligence with this stubborn sapling!

Lisa Worthey Smith

Winter Will Come

S erving as a backdrop behind the waterfall of our little pond is a trellis which is beautifully clothed with a clematis vine. After the snow clears and the iris begin to bloom, the clematis begins its preparation for winter by celebrating spring. Its contribution to the "spring party" is production of delicate, deep-blue flowers open wide for all to see. The lovely blue-bloomers perfectly complement the white and yellow daffodils which, by that time, are in full bloom. Don't you just love how God perfectly coordinates His Creation?

The "early bird" butterflies flutter by for a visit, soon joined by hummingbirds, bees, and lizards. I must admit the lizards are probably seeking a bee snack or some other slow-moving insect rather than the

beauty of the blooms. As the summer goes by, a dozen or more blooms, each having a multitude of visitors, will come and go, each having a moment of glory and opportunity to show the world their beauty.

When summer is over and fall has taken the stage, the daffodil and clematis blooms are gone. The iris and daffodils leave little wads of seed pods, effective and functional, but not particularly attractive. The clematis, however, "shows out" (Southern for "doing more than expected") with fantastic, fuzzy little gems of seed pods, each of which is just as spectacular as their former bloom.

Even though different from the beauty of the flower, they are each still full of potential life. These delightfully fancy hands-full of fluff lightly hold on to several seeds in their center. With the first good wind and rain, you know what will happen. It will be fruitful and multiply, spreading seeds that will replicate this pretty little vine with little vine "babies." As the original vine grows old, the babies will grow up and so the cycle continues.

We, like the flowers, live for a season and then we die.

In my efforts to learn and record some of our family history, I have found many, many people who lived and died long before I was born. Often all I have is a name, birth date, date of death, and where they lived. Their parents and children may be listed, but very often I don't learn much about the dash between their birth date and date of death.

Sometimes there will be a tidbit of interesting information. For instance, one ten-year-old relative died in 1887 after being hit by a limb falling from a tree that he and a friend cut while trying to capture a raccoon - a sad legacy of a life ending tragically.

I found this relative's obituary written in a scrapbook for posterity.

"Joseph Terry departed this life on the 18th day of September 1881 in the 75th year of his age leaving a wife, 8 children, a large number

of grandchildren and hosts of friends to mourn his death. He died on the Lord's Day and began talking first the night before about 10 o'clock.

The day he died he called his family into Rev. G. W. Thrasher, and said he thanked God that he was not afraid to die. He then said to his wife, "Well, old woman, you have been a faithful soldier of the cross and it won't be long 'til we meet to part no more."

He said to those of his children that had made peace with God, "Be faithful to the end." To those of his children that had made no profession he turned and exhorted them to seek the better way, and obtained a promise from each of them to try and meet him in heaven.

He left comforting evidences that he was at peace with his Savior. He was buried on the 20th, when wife, children, grandchildren neighbors and friends met at the grave to take the last look at a kind husband, a loving father, a true friend, a good neighbor and a noble citizen.

His funeral sermon was preached on the first Sunday in October by Brother G. W. Thrasher from Thessalonians Chapter 4 verse 18. His spirit is now at rest."

A note written as a post script reads *"He tried to sing "Oh, Carry Me Away on Your Lily-White Wings" but couldn't then he tried to whistle it and couldn't so Frank Cheatham sang it for him."*

Now that, my friends, is an obituary! It is a wonderful legacy remaining of a life lived well - seeds, if you will, for future generations. Some funerals are like that, just beautiful pictures of Christian lives lived with hope, courage, and ongoing encouragement to follow their footsteps.

It seems to me that life in my Father's world follows patterns, and that like the flowers, our lives also have a time to bloom and a time to fade away. We each have a date of birth and a date of death, but what will we leave behind? What will our seed pod be like?

I've had the tremendous blessing of friends whose lives were bright flowers to all who met them. When they left this world, the funeral was spectacular. We all remember and celebrate a Christ-like life lived with hope, courage, and encouragement which will continue long after the life is over, a direct result of the seeds they left.

We all have that opportunity. How we live out our lifetimes, in good times or trials, can build or break another's faith. How we proclaim our faith will determine the number and type of seeds we produce, or whether we simply leave dried up blooms. Regardless of how successful our careers were, how many "toys" we accumulated, how extravagant our wardrobe, or how meticulously manicured our yards, we will leave this earth.

The question is, what will we leave behind? Those whose lives we have touched will be our lasting legacy, the seeds that will take root and grow for another season.

Lessons to Remember
From the Garden

❖ The Master Gardener does not allow His bloomers to be strangled.

❖ The rules of the harvest remain true. We reap what we sow.

❖ We should bloom where we are planted.

❖ Things change. Be willing to be moved. It may for your good.

❖ All caskets are temporary.

❖ Fill the garden with a pleasing fragrance.

❖ When it rains, drink.

❖ Learn to discern predators.

❖ A little pruning might be good for you.

❖ Accept that winter comes. Prepare.

Reader's Guide

Τhis guide is divided into a few topics that are often subjects of discussions. The purpose of this guide is to give you Scripture with which you can accurately find answers to these probing questions in either an individual or group setting. It is recommended that you read the selected passages and the surrounding text for accurate context and the best understanding of the truth. For your convenience selected Scripture is printed out in the New American Standard Version translation of the Holy Bible.

The more you study, the more questions you may have. Don't worry, that is a good thing! It means you are hungry for the truth, so let this be a starting point for even deeper study.

You are to be commended for your diligence to study and learn. The next step will be for you to share. I encourage you to share the truths you have discovered with someone today. You might be the very one God uses to reach one who desperately needs to hear the truth!

Precious one, I pray God blesses you in this journey and that His light shines brightly within you always!

God and Creation

"O LORD, our Lord,
how majestic is Your name in all the earth,
Who have displayed Your splendor above the heavens!
From the mouth of infants and nursing babes
You have established strength
because of Your adversaries,
to make the enemy and the revengeful cease.

When I consider Your heavens,
the work of Your fingers,
the moon and the stars,
which You have ordained;
what is man that You take thought of him, and
the son of man that You care for him?

Yet You have made him a little lower than God, and
You crown him with glory and majesty!
You make him to rule over the works of Your hands;
You have put all things under his feet,
all sheep and oxen,
and also the beasts of the field,
the birds of the heavens and the fish of the sea,
whatever passes through the paths of the seas.
O LORD, our Lord,
how majestic is Your name in all the earth!"
Psalm 8:1-9

<u>Study Questions</u>

1. Whose hands created the moon, stars and the heavens?

2. So, Whose majesty is displayed in Creation?

3. What is our relationship to Him?

4. What is our obligation to His Creation?

5. Does anything we do result in glory or majesty?

More about Creation

"For the wrath of God is revealed from heaven against all ungodliness and
> *unrighteousness of men*
> *who suppress the truth in unrighteousness,*
> *because that which is known about God*
> *is evident within them;*
> *for God made it evident to them.*
> *For since the creation of the world*
> *His invisible attributes,*
> *His eternal power and divine nature,*
> *have been clearly seen,*
> *being understood through what has been made,*
> *so that they are without excuse."*

Romans 1:18-20

Study questions

1. If God is invisible, what evidence do we have that He is real?

2. Explain the phrase *"been clearly seen."*

3. What will those who suppress this truth experience? (Hint the first five words in the passage.)

4. What defense or excuse will be available?

God and Wisdom,
Knowledge and Understanding

Consider the following passage regarding wisdom, knowledge, and understanding that comes from God. Although written in its entirety, this Scripture is structured in a way that illuminates certain topics and thoughts. Read it through, and see if you can spot some lists that could be made from this passage. Then, answer the questions that follow.

"How blessed
 is the man who finds wisdom and
 the man who gains understanding.
 For
   her profit is better than the profit of silver and
   her gain better than fine gold.
She is more precious than jewels; and
   nothing you desire compares with her.
   Long life is in her right hand;
     in her left hand are riches and honor.
   Her ways are pleasant ways and
   all her paths are peace.
   She is a tree of life
     to those who take hold of her, and
     happy are all who hold her fast.
The LORD
 by wisdom founded the earth,
 by understanding He established the heavens.
 By His knowledge the deeps were broken up and
 the skies drip with dew.

My son,

let them not vanish from your sight;
keep sound wisdom and discretion,

so they will be

life to your soul and
adornment to your neck.

Then

you will walk in your way securely and
your foot will not stumble.
When you lie down,

you will not be afraid;
when you lie down,
your sleep will be sweet.

Do not be afraid

of sudden fear nor
of the onslaught of the wicked when it comes;
for

the LORD

will be your confidence and
will keep your foot from being caught."
Proverbs 3:13-26

Your notes

Study questions

1. What is having God's wisdom and understanding compared to having gold, silver, and jewels?

2. How powerful is this wisdom? (How did God do use it?)

3. What should we do with such wisdom and why?

4. When we have this wisdom and understanding, what happens to

   our fear?

   our day to day walk?

Why? (When studying, always look for terms of conclusion; words like *because, for, thus, as a result*).

For the LORD ...

Lisa Worthey Smith

More about Wisdom, Knowledge and Understanding

Four young Jewish men, Daniel, Hananiah, Mishael and Azariah (you might be more familiar with the last three by their Babylonian names, Shadrach, Meshach and Abed-nego) were captured by the Babylonian King Nebuchadnezzar. They were chosen for service to the King's court because of their youth and intelligence. How did they come to have such intelligence that was so easily recognized?

"As for these four youths,
God gave them knowledge and intelligence
in every branch of literature and wisdom;
Daniel even understood all kinds of visions and dreams."
Daniel 1:17

"For the LORD gives wisdom;
from His mouth come knowledge and understanding.
He stores up sound wisdom for the upright".
Proverbs 2:6-7a

"But if any of you lacks wisdom,
let him ask of God,
who gives to all generously and without reproach, and
it will be given to him."
James 1:5

Summarize where, and how wisdom is found, and its value to us.

Suffering

I f God is able to create the universe and give us wisdom, knowledge and understanding, why does He allow us to suffer? **First, remember that Christ suffered …**
After the disciples witnessed Jesus feed thousands with a few pieces of bread and a couple of fish they had questions for Him. Jesus told them that He *"must suffer many things and be rejected by the elders and chief priests and scribes, and be killed and be raised up on the third day. And He was saying to them all, "If anyone wishes to come after Me, he must deny himself, and take up his cross daily and follow Me."* Luke 9:22-23

Study Questions

1. Was Jesus surprised about His crucifixion that was to come?

2. What did He tell them about what they should expect as followers of Him?

3. Do you think He meant that this suffering was to be expected only by the disciples in the time of Jesus? Before you answer, read what Paul reminded the church at Philippi in the Scripture below (years after Christ was crucified).

"For to you it has been granted for Christ's sake,
not only to believe in Him,
but also to suffer for His sake,
experiencing the same conflict which you saw in me, and now hear
to be in me."
Philippians 1:29-30

4. Did you notice that it was not "demanded" that they/we suffer, but rather *"granted"?* This word is associated with a gift. Its root comes from the same word as grace – something that gives joy and is given from lovingkindness. How can suffering be a gift given from love?

More on Jesus' Suffering

Jesus' words from His Sermon on the Mount (the underlining and bold print have been added):

"Blessed are those who have been <u>persecuted</u>
<u>for the sake of righteousness,</u>
for theirs is the kingdom of heaven.
"Blessed are you when <u>people insult you</u>
<u>and persecute you,</u>
<u>and falsely say all kinds of evil against you</u>
<u>because of Me.</u>
"Rejoice and be glad,
for your reward in heaven is great;
for in the same way they persecuted the prophets
who were before you."
Matthew 10:5-13

1. In the <u>underlined</u> text, what type suffering is discussed here?

2. What then should our response be?
R_____ and be g_____

In **bold** print, when we endure this type suffering what will we receive, and when will we receive it? (Did you notice the term of conclusion?)

An eternal perspective...

"For you have not received a spirit of slavery
leading to fear again, but
you have received a spirit of adoption as sons
by which we cry out, "Abba! Father!"
The Spirit Himself testifies with our spirit that
we are children of God, and
if children, heirs also,
heirs of God and
fellow heirs with Christ,
if indeed we suffer with Him
so that we may also be glorified with Him.
For I consider that the sufferings of this present time
are not worthy to be compared with
the glory that is to be revealed to us."
Romans 8:15-18

When we become Christians, we call God our Father, just as Jesus did. That makes us joint heirs with Jesus to all that is owned by God. How does any temporary suffering we endure compare to that inheritance?

Rejoicing...

"Beloved,

do not be surprised at the fiery ordeal among you,

which comes upon you for your testing,

as though some strange thing

were happening to you;

but to the degree that you share the sufferings of Christ, keep on
rejoicing,

so that also at the revelation of His glory

you may rejoice with exultation.

If you are reviled for the name of Christ,

you are blessed,

because the Spirit of glory and of God rests on you. Make sure that
none of you suffers

as a murderer,

or thief,

or evildoer,

or a troublesome meddler;

but if anyone suffers as a Christian,

he is not to be ashamed,

but is to glorify God in this name."

1 Peter 4:13-16

Study Questions

1. Christ was not surprised that He suffered. Should we be
   surprised?

2. What should we do?

Keep on_____

Not be_____

3. Why?
   so that_____

   you may_____

   you are_____ because

4. What is the warning?

An example of suffering…

Joseph, a favorite son of his father, was sold by his brothers into slavery in a foreign country (Egypt) as a teenager.

"Now Joseph had been taken down to Egypt;
and Potiphar, an Egyptian officer of Pharaoh,
the captain of the bodyguard,
bought him from the Ishmaelites,
who had taken him down there.
The LORD *was with Joseph,*
so he became a successful man.
And he was in the house of his master, the Egyptian. Now his master saw
that the LORD *was with him and*
how the LORD *caused all that he did to prosper*
in his hand.
So Joseph found favor in his sight and
became his personal servant; and
he made him overseer over his house, and
all that he owned he put in his charge.
It came about that from the time he made him overseer in his house and
over all that he owned,
the LORD *blessed the Egyptian's house*
on account of Joseph;
thus the LORD'S *blessing was upon all that he owned, in the house and in the field."*
Genesis 39:1-5

<u>Study questions from Genesis 39:1-5</u>

1. Even though he was in slavery, Who was with him and caused him to be successful?

2. What caused attention to be drawn to Joseph?

3. What resulted from that for Joseph? (Look for the terms of conclusion.)

Many years later, Joseph spoke these words to his brothers; *"As for you, you meant evil against me, but God meant it for good*
in order to bring about this present result,
to preserve many people alive.
"So therefore, do not be afraid;
I will provide for you and your little ones."
So he comforted them and spoke kindly to them." Genesis 50:20-22

4. Why did God allow him to undergo this?

In order to_____

to_____

His attitude toward his brothers, who had such hatred toward him, is exemplary. If he could see the hand of God at work in such circumstances and trust in Him still, without falling into self-pity, what example does that leave us?

Your thoughts

Lisa Worthey Smith

Reasons for suffering...

*"Blessed be the God and
Father of our Lord Jesus Christ,
the Father of mercies and
God of all comfort,
who comforts us in all our affliction
so that we will be able to comfort those
who are in any affliction
with the comfort
with which we ourselves are comforted by God.
For just as the sufferings of Christ
are ours in abundance,
so also our comfort is abundant through Christ.
But if we are afflicted,
it is for your comfort and salvation;
or if we are comforted,
it is for your comfort,
which is effective in the patient enduring
of the same sufferings which we also suffer; and
our hope for you is firmly grounded,
knowing that as you are sharers of our sufferings,
so also you are sharers of our comfort."*
  2   Corinthians 1:3-7

Using the passage from 2 Corinthians, consider the following questions.

1. What does God give us when we suffer?

2. How much does He give?

3. Why does He give it?

4. What do we have to share?

Another reason God allows suffering...

"You shall remember all the way which the L*ORD* *your God has led you in the wilderness these forty years,*

> *that He might humble you,*
>> *testing you,*
>> *to know what was in your heart,*
>>> *whether you would keep His commandments or not.*

"He humbled you and
let you be hungry, and
fed you with manna

>> *which you did not know,*
>> *nor did your fathers know,*

> *that He might make you understand*

>> *that man does not live*
>>> *by bread alone, but*
>> *man lives*

>>> *by everything that proceeds out of the mouth*
>>> *of the* L*ORD*.

"Your clothing did not wear out on you, nor
did your foot swell these forty years.

"Thus

>> *you are to know in your heart that the* L*ORD* *your God was*
> *disciplining you*
>> *just as a man disciplines his son.*

"Therefore, you shall keep the commandments
> *of the* L*ORD* *your God,*

>> *to walk in His ways and*
>> *to fear Him."*

Deuteronomy 8:2-6

Study questions from Deuteronomy 8:2-6

1. Were the "Israelites wandering on their own" or being "led" in the wilderness for forty years?

2. What lesson did their hunger and lack of new clothing teach them about God?

3. Where then, should be our focus?

4. What is the connection between our "heart" and His "commandments"?

5. Find the term of conclusion "Therefore". What is the desired result of God allowing this wilderness experience?

From the first sentence, it appears God sometimes uses humility to teach us. Have you experienced a lesson in humility?

Humility

He has told you, O man, what is good;
And what does the LORD require of you
But to do justice, to love kindness,
And to walk humbly with your God? Micah 6:8

"Do nothing from selfishness or empty conceit,
but with humility of mind
regard one another as
more important than yourselves;
do not merely look out for your own personal interests,
but also for the interests of others.
Have this attitude in yourselves
which was also in Christ Jesus,
who, although He existed in the form of God,
did not regard equality with God a thing to be grasped, but emptied
Himself,
taking the form of a bond-servant, and
being made in the likeness of men.
Being found in appearance as a man,
He humbled Himself by becoming obedient
to the point of death,
even death on a cross.
For this reason also,
God highly exalted Him, and
bestowed on Him the name which is above every name, so that at
the name of Jesus EVERY KNEE WILL BOW, of those who are in heaven
and

on earth and
under the earth, and
that every tongue will confess that
Jesus Christ is Lord,
to the glory of God the Father.
So then, my beloved,
just as you have always obeyed,
not as in my presence only,
but now much more in my absence,
work out your salvation with fear and trembling;
for it is God who is at work in you,
both to will and to work for His good pleasure." Philippians 2:3-13

Study questions

1. From the first sentence of the Philippians passage, what two things are we NOT to do?

❖ _____

❖ _____

2. In contrast, what are we TO do?

3. From the next sentence, whose example should we follow?

4. Notice that His humility led Him to obedience. To death. How did God regard His humility and obedience?

❖ Highly_____

❖ Bestowed_____
So that, at the name of Jesus
Every_____
Whose knees will bow?
Every_____

5. So, what is the conclusion? Obey, and work out your salvation with fear and trembling
for_____

_____

_____for His good pleasure.

"For thus says the high and exalted One
Who lives forever,
whose name is Holy,
"I dwell on a high and holy place, And
also with the contrite and lowly of spirit
In order to revive the spirit of the lowly
And to revive the heart of the contrite."
Isaiah 57:15

6. Where are the two places listed where we can find God?

7. What benefit comes from Him to the lowly and contrite?

Your notes regarding humility;

W ere you expecting **THE END**? Surprise! This is not the end. While I commend your diligence *(good job!)* in this brief study, I now pray this is a starting point. I pray you are eager to dig even deeper into studying the Bible.

It can seem a daunting task to study the entire Bible. While some people start at the very beginning and read from Genesis all the way through Revelation, it can be very helpful to just read and study one book of the Bible at a time.

I recommend you begin in the New Testament with the gospel of John. There, you will have an up close and personal meeting with God in the flesh, Jesus.

Read it slowly and carefully.

Read it several times over the course of a few days.

Look for repeated phrases, and make lists of what you learn (about the people, about what Jesus said about why He came, etc.). By implementing the same techniques, you just used in the Reader's Guide, you can now explore the vast truths in the Bible for yourself!

Summary

Look at that brave little leaf reaching over the rushing water. Do you think he told his mom that "I can't do that! I'm scared! I'll fall in! I'm not strong enough!" I don't know, maybe he did. I would have.

But look at what he was able to accomplish. This one little leaf is

changing the course of the flow of the waterfall. Just one little leaf.

You and I are also making a difference in the lives of those around us every day. A word of encouragement may seem like a tiny leaf in the course of a lifetime, but it could make a big difference to someone whose life is rushing over a waterfall.

A difficult time in your life could be used by God to encourage someone else to carry on with courage and faith. A simple story of a time when God has been evident in your life might be just the thing God uses to draw that one more person to Himself today.

I have confidence that you can do it, because we both know you have been designed and equipped to bloom exactly where you are. Bloom!

We don't have to be afraid. He is with us. Look around you every day - He is there. His hand is evident in all of Creation. He is working. The more we recognize Him, the more His peace, knowledge, and security works in us. When hard times come, know that He will help you through them. You never know, He might even send that help wrapped up in a little hummingbird package!

- *Please consider leaving a review on Amazon.com. Your reviews help others decide if the book is right for them. Thank you!*

- *Follow the Facebook page for Oscar the Extraordinary Hummingbird for more pictures of hummingbirds.*

About the Author

L ong time Bible student and teacher, **Lisa Worthey Smith** has been called "The Parable Teacher." She often uses the small and simple to illustrate the profound—especially pointing readers to fresh ways to apply Scripture in their lives, and to see the evidence of the hand God all around them.

Lisa and her husband are empty nesting in north Alabama, where she writes, tends her hummingbird garden, and serves as president of the local Word Weavers chapter.

Other books by Lisa Worthey Smith

The Wisdom Tree

Set in the Garden of Gethsemane, the little olive tree tells of his life growing up in the time of Jesus, nurtured by the Master of the Garden, his roots guided and encouraged by an unseen worm, and finally interacting with Teacher. Especially that one tragic night. His life lessons echo themes of "trust, believe, and look up."

Reviews -

- Karen, *"Like reading Max Lucado."*
- Julia Wilson The Christian Bookahaolic, The Wisdom Tree *"is right up there with C. S. Lewis's Narnia!"*

The Ground Kisser

By Thanh Duong Boyer with
Lisa Worthey Smith

The award-winning memoir of a Vietnamese refugee who set out to find freedom for herself and her family. After the fall of Saigon, at barely twelve years old, she boarded a boat headed to find freedom in Australia. Pirates attacked her boat and stole that dream. More than one obstacle tried to snatch her life before she made her way to the USA.

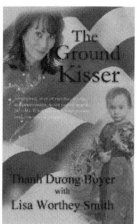

- Legendary talk-show host, **Barry Farber** dubbed her a *"Ground Kisser"* when he heard of her profound gratitude to live in the USA.
- *Should be required reading for every student ... every American."* Hon. **Tommy Battle**, Mayor Huntsville, AL

References:

[i]*New American Standard Bible: 1995 update.* 1995 (Psalm 19:14). The Lockman Foundation: LaHabra, CA
[ii]Ibid, (Matthew 10:29).

[iii] Ibid, (Genesis 1:26, Psalm 8:6-8).

[iv] Ibid, (Matthew 11:28, 29, Isaiah 41:10).

[v] Ibid, (John 10:28, 29).

[vi] Ibid, (Isaiah 64:6).

[vii] Ibid, (Isaiah 61:10).

[viii] Ibid, (Ephesians 4:24-26, Romans 6:4).

[ix] Ibid, (Psalm 139:13-16, Isaiah 44:24).

[x] Ibid, (Luke 12:27).

[xi] Ibid, (Matthew 7:11).

[xii] Ibid, (James 1:5).

[xiii] Ibid, (Proverbs 16:32).

[xiv] Ibid, (1 Thessalonians 5:18).

[xv] Ibid, (Philippians 4:7).

[xvi] Ibid, (Revelation 8:1-4).

[xvii] Ibid, (Esther 4:14).

[xviii] Ibid, (2 Corinthians 1:3-5).

[xix] Ibid, (2 Corinthians 12:9).

[xx] Ibid, (Proverbs 14:12).

[xxi] Ibid, (Isaiah 59:2).

[xxii] Ibid, (Philippians 3:8–11).

[xxiii] Ibid, (John 14:6).

[xxiv] Ibid, (Deuteronomy 31:6, 1 Chronicles 28:20).

[xxv] Ibid, (Romans 6:23).

[xxvi] Ibid, (Philippians 3:8).

[xxvii] Ibid, (Hebrews 13:20, 21).

[xxviii] Ibid, (2 Corinthians 12:9).

[xxix] Ibid, (2 Corinthians 4:17).

[xxx] Ibid, (Romans 8:28).

[xxxi] Ibid, (1 John 5:4-5).
[xxxii] Ibid, (2 Corinthians 2:14-16).
[xxxiii] Ibid, (John 10:10).
[xxxiv] Ibid, (Psalm 119:11).
[xxxv] Ibid, (James 1:2-4).
[xxxvi] Ibid, (1 Peter 1:6-9).
[xxxvii] Ibid, (Proverbs 22:6).

Made in the USA
Lexington, KY
13 November 2019